The original

ŠEVČÍK

VIOLIN STUDIES

STUDIES PREPARATORY TO THE SHAKE & DEVELOPMENT IN DOUBLE-STOPPING

TRILLER-VORSTUDIEN

EXERCICES POUR PRÉPARER ET DÉVELOPPER LE TRILLE

Op. 7 Part 1

T0056423

BOSWORTH

Triller Uebungen
in der 1. Lage.

ESERCIZI SUL TRILLO
nella 1ª posizione.

Traduzione italiana di M. PELISSIER.

Exercices de trille
dans la 1re position.

Trilková cvičení
v 1. poloze.

Trill exercises
in the first position.

УПРАЖНЕНІЯ ВЪ ТРЕЛИ
въ 1ой позиціи.

1.

Halbton: 1-2 Finger.
Diese Uebung ist auf folgende sechs Arten zu spielen:

Semitono: 1-2 dito
Studiare questo esercizio nelle sei maniere seguenti:

Půlton: 1.-2. prst.
Cvičení toto budiž hráno následujícími šesti způsoby:

Demi-ton: 1.-2. doigt.
On travaillera cet exercice des six manières suivantes:

Полутонъ: 1-2 палецъ.
Это упражненіе должно быть исполняемо слѣдующими шестью способами:

Semitone: 1.-2. finger.
Practise this exercise in the six following ways:

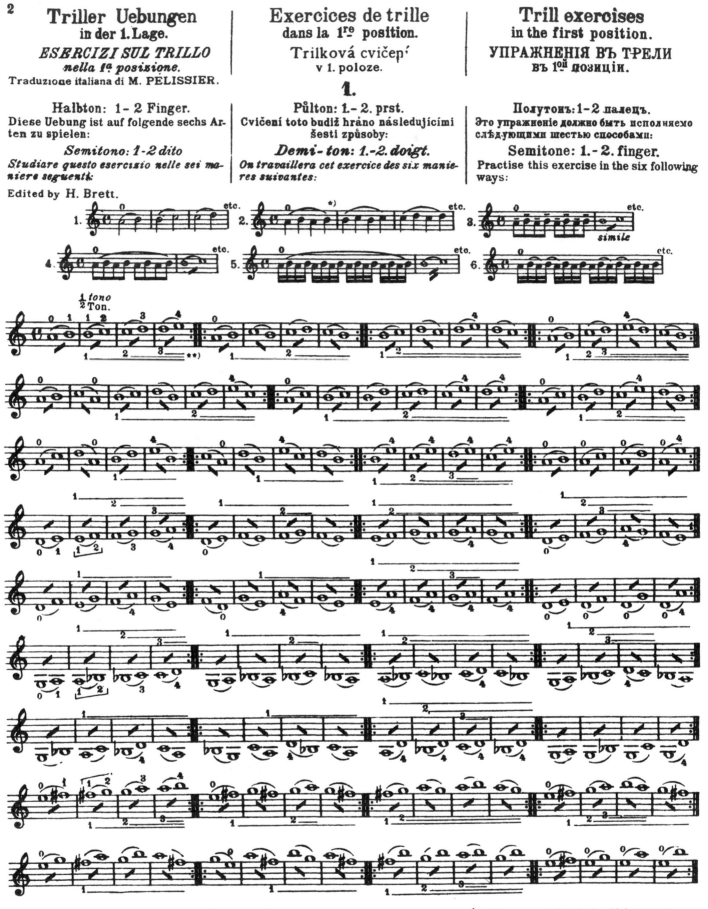

Edited by H. Brett.

*) Den Finger hoch heben und denselben kräftig und gleichmässig auf die Saite fallen lassen.
*) *Alzare le dita e lasciarle cadere sulla corda con forza ed eguaglianza.*
**) Die Finger bleiben auf der Saite liegen.
**) *Lasciare le dita ferme.*

*) *Bien lever le doigt et le laisser tomber sur la corde avec force et avec égalité.*
*) Úder prstu, vysoko zvednutého, musí býti silný a stejnoměrný.
**) *Laisser les doigts en place.*
**) Prsty zůstávají na struně.

*) The finger to be lifted up high and let fall on the string with force and with equality.
*) Ударъ пальцемъ, высоко поднятымъ, долженъ быть сильный и равномѣрный.
**) The fingers to be kept down on the string.
**) Пальцы остаются на струнѣ.

2.

Semitono: 2-3 dito.
Halbton: 2.-3. Finger.

Půlton: 2.-3. prst.
Demi-ton: 2.-3. doigt.

Полутонъ: 2-3 палецъ.
Semitone: 2.-3. finger.

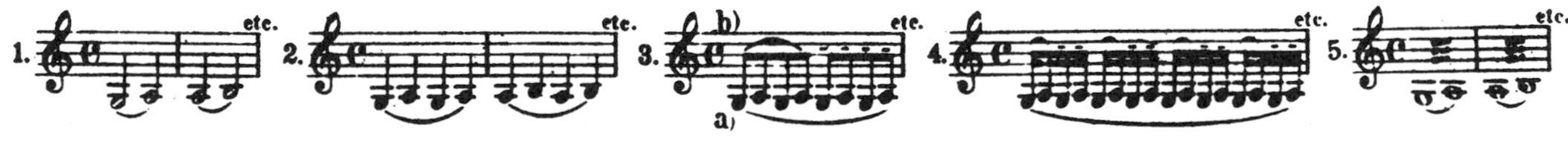

*) *Lasciare le dita ferme vedi Nº 1.*
*) Die Finger liegen lassen, s. Nº 1.

*) Prsty ponechavají se na místě, v. Nº 1.
*) *Laisser les doigts en place, voir Nº 1.*

*) Пальцы остаются на мѣстѣ, см. Nº 1.
*) The fingers to be kept down. See Nº 1.

3.

Semitono: 0-1; 3-4 dito. | Půltony: 0-1, 3.-4. prst. | Полутоны: 0-1. и 3-4 палецъ.

Halbtöne: 0-1., 3.-4. Finger. | *Demi-tons: 0-1., 3.-4. doigt.* | Semitones: 0-1 3.-4. finger.

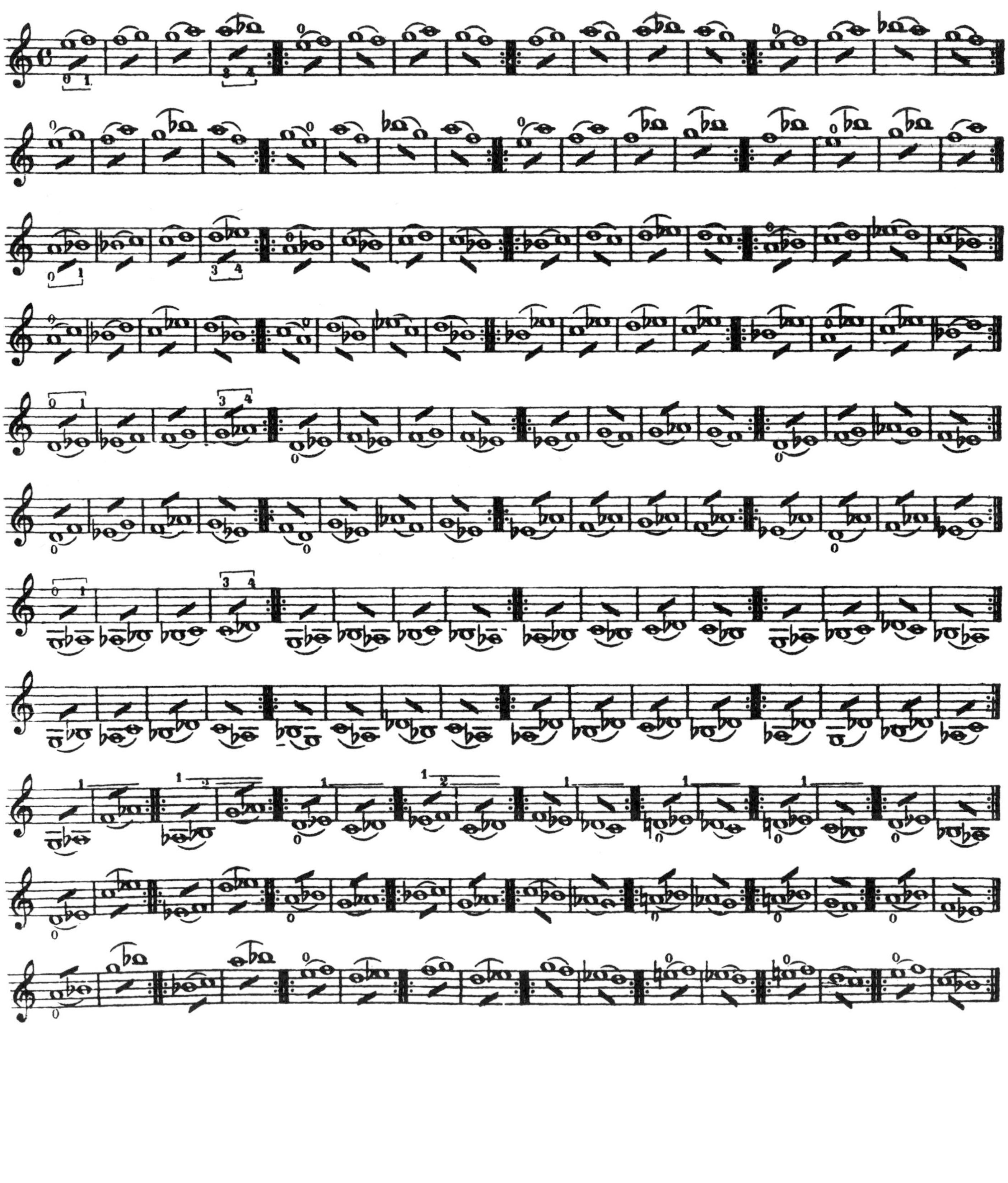

4.

Accidenti.
Scala cromatica
Versetzungszeichen.
Chromatische Tonfolge.

Posuvky.
Chromatická stupnice.
Signes de deplacement.
Gamme chromatique.

Знаки альтерацін.
Хроматическая гамма.
Accidentals.
Chromatic passages.

5

Scale. Tonleitern. | Stupnice. *Gammes.* | Таммы. Scales.

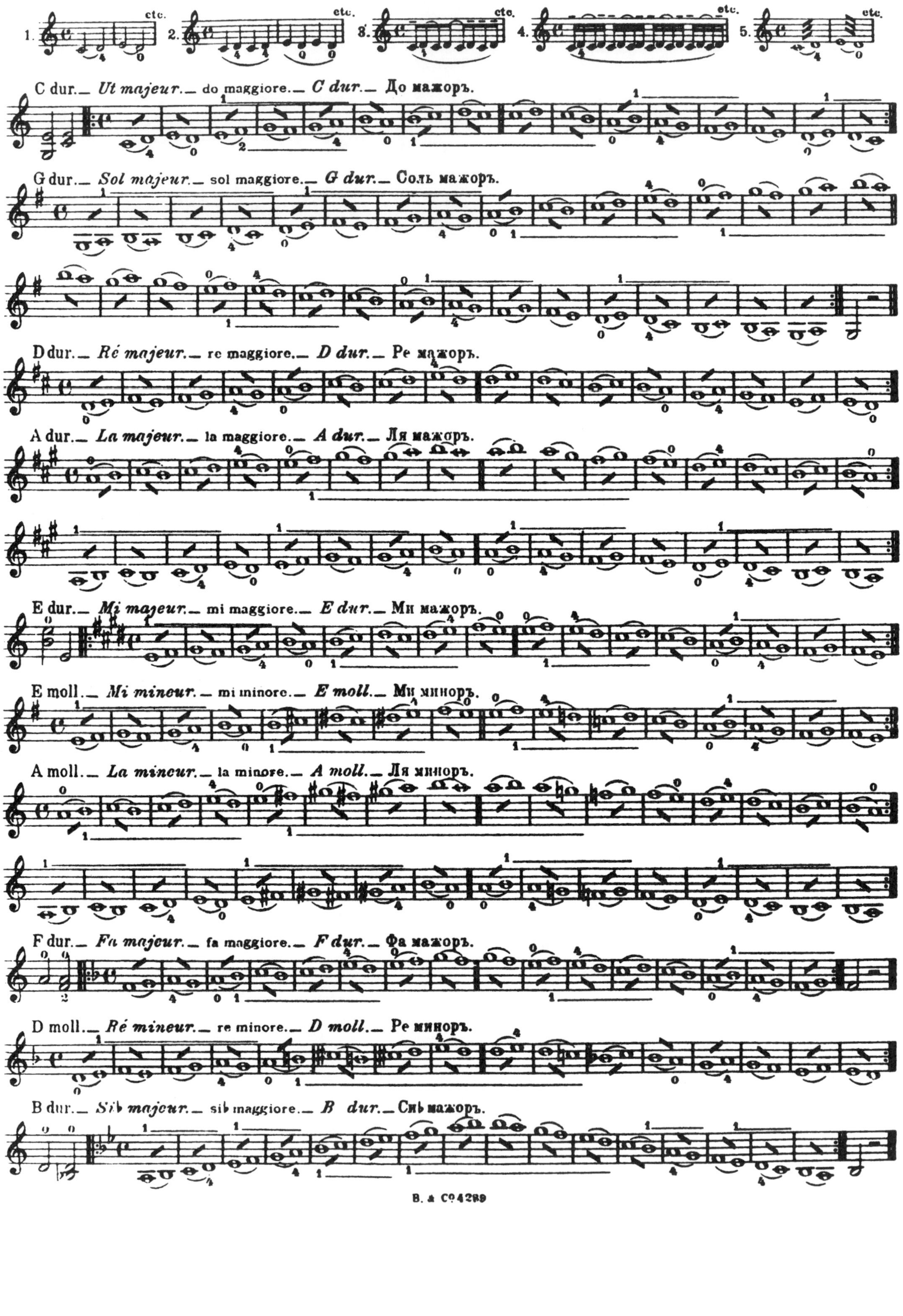
1.
2.
3.
4.
5.
etc.
C dur. — *Ut majeur.* — do maggiore. — *C dur.* — До мажоръ.
G dur. — *Sol majeur.* — sol maggiore. — *G dur.* — Соль мажоръ.
D dur. — *Ré majeur.* — re maggiore. — *D dur.* — Ре мажоръ.
A dur. — *La majeur.* — la maggiore. — *A dur.* — Ля мажоръ.
E dur. — *Mi majeur.* — mi maggiore. — *E dur.* — Ми мажоръ.
E moll. — *Mi mineur.* — mi minore. — *E moll.* — Ми миноръ.
A moll. — *La mineur.* — la minore. — *A moll.* — Ля миноръ.
F dur. — *Fa majeur.* — fa maggiore. — *F dur.* — Фа мажоръ.
D moll. — *Ré mineur.* — re minore. — *D moll.* — Ре миноръ.
B dur. — *Si♭ majeur.* — si♭ maggiore. — *B dur.* — Си♭ мажоръ.

G moll. _ Sol mineur. _ sol minore. _ G moll. _ Соль миноръ.
Es dur. _ Mi♭ majeur. _ mi ♭ maggiore. _ Es dur. _ Ми ♭ мажоръ.
C moll. _ Ut mineur. _ do minore. _ C moll. _ До миноръ.
As dur. _ La ♭ majeur. _ la ♭ maggiore. _ As dur. _ Ля ♭ мажоръ.
F moll. _ Fa mineur. _ fa minore. _ F moll. _ Фа миноръ.
Des dur. _ Re ♭ majeur. _ re ♭ maggiore. _ Des dur. _ Ре ♭ мажоръ.
B moll. _ Si♭ mineur. _ si ♭ minore. _ B moll. _ Си ♭ мажоръ.
Ges dur. _ Sol ♭ majeur. _ sol ♭ maggiore. _ Ges dur. _ Соль ♭ мажоръ.
Es moll. _ Mi♭ mineur. _ mi ♭ minore. _ Es moll. _ Ми ♭ мажоръ.
H dur. _ Si majeur. _ si maggiore. _ H dur. _ Си мажоръ.
H moll. _ Si mineur. _ si minore. _ H moll. Си миноръ.
Fis moll. _ Fa ♯ mineur. _ fa ♯ minore. _ Fis moll. _ Фа ♯ миноръ.
Cis moll. _ Ut ♯ mineur. _ do ♯ minore. _ Cis moll. _ До ♯ миноръ.
Gis moll. _ Sol ♯ mineur. _ sol ♯ minore. _ Gis moll. Соль ♯ миноръ.

6.

Accordi perfetti maggiori. | Trojzvuky tvrdé. | Мажорныя трезвучія.

Dur-Dreiklänge. | *Des accords parfaits majeurs.* | Major triads.

Des dur. – Ré♭ majeur. – re♭ maggiore. – Des dur. – Ре♭ мажоръ.
Ges dur. – Sol♭ majeur. – sol♭ maggiore. Ges dur. – Соль♭ мажоръ.
H dur. – Si majeur. – si maggiore. – H dur. – Си мажоръ.

7.

Accordi perfetti minori.
Quinta aumentata e quarta diminuita.

Moll-Dreiklänge.

Uebermässige Quinte und verminderte Quarte.

Trojzvuky měkké.
Zvětšená kvinta a zmenšená kvarta.

Des accords parfaits mineurs.

La quinte augmentée et la quarte diminuée

Минорныя трезвучія.
Увеличенная квинта и уменьшенная кварта.

Minor triads.

The augmented fifth and the diminished fourth.

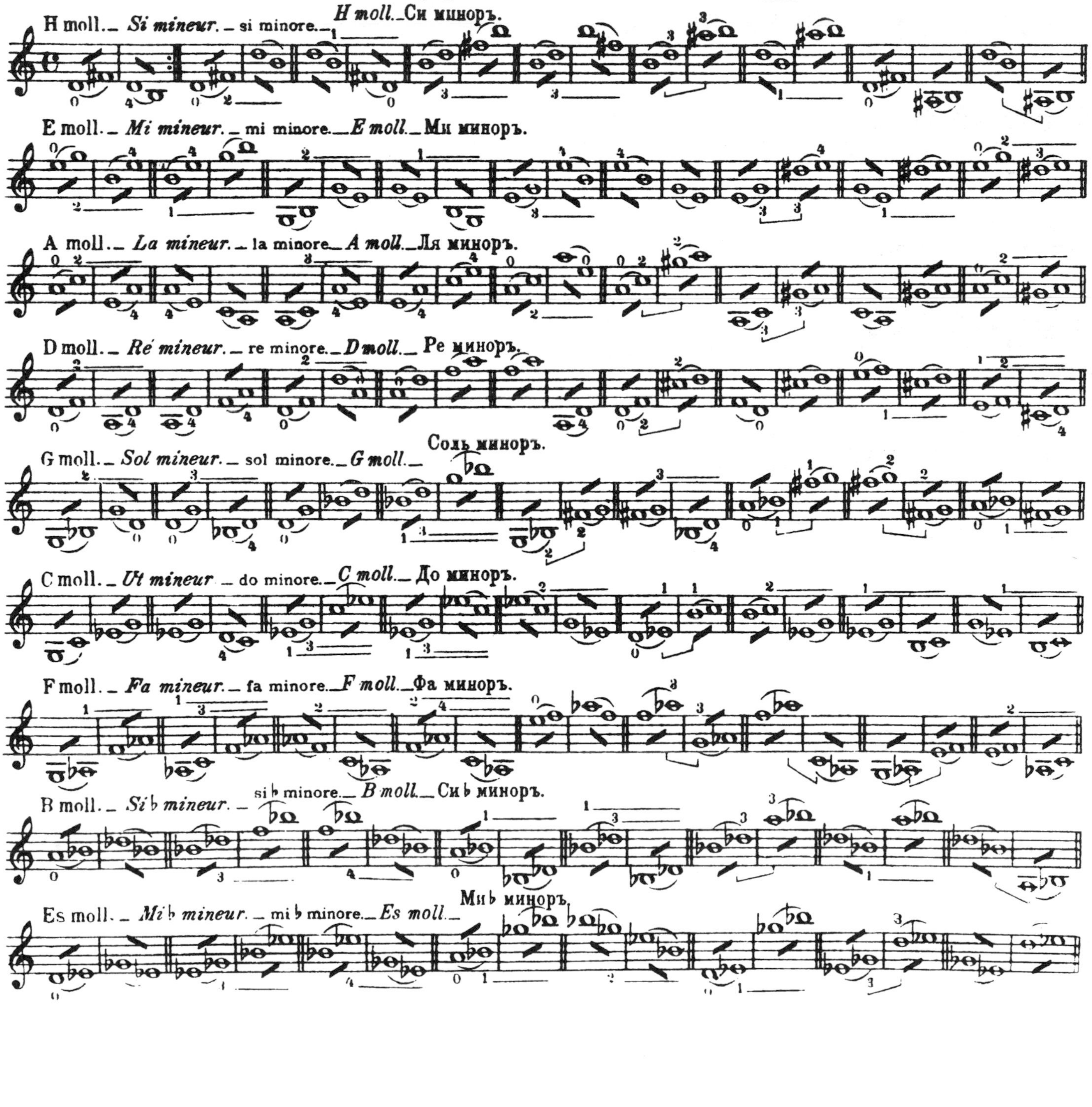
H moll. – Si mineur. – si minore. – H moll. – Си миноръ.
E moll. – Mi mineur. – mi minore. – E moll. – Ми миноръ.
A moll. – La mineur. – la minore – A moll. – Ля миноръ.
D moll. – Ré mineur. – re minore. – D moll. – Ре миноръ.
G moll. – Sol mineur. – sol minore. – G moll. – Соль миноръ.
C moll. – Ut mineur – do minore. – C moll. – До миноръ.
F moll. – Fa mineur. – fa minore. – F moll. – Фа миноръ.
B moll. – Si♭ mineur. – si♭ minore. – B moll. – Си♭ миноръ.
Es moll. – Mi♭ mineur. – mi♭ minore. – Es moll. – Ми♭ миноръ.

As moll. — *La ♭ mineur.* — la ♭ minore. — *As moll.* — Ля ♭ миноръ.

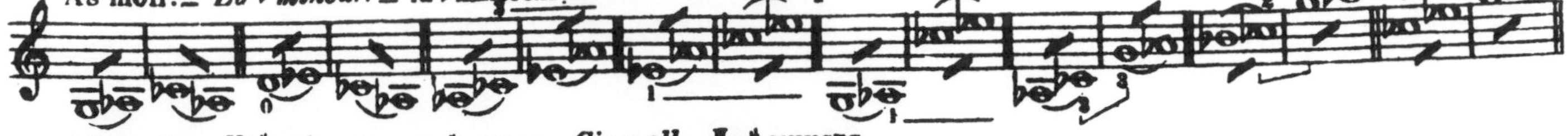

Cis moll. — *Ut ♯ mineur.* — do ♯ minore. — *Cis moll.* — До ♯ миноръ.

Fis moll. — *Fa ♯ mineur.* — fa ♯ minore. — *Fis moll.* — Фа ♯ миноръ.

8.

Accordo perfetto in tutti i toni maggiori e minori.
Dreiklang in allen Dur- und Molltonarten.

Trojzvuk ve všech tvrdých a měkkých toninách.
***Accord parfait** dans tous les tons majeurs et mineurs.*

Трезвучіе во всѣхъ мажорныхъ и минорныхъ тональностяхъ.
The triad in all major and minor keys.

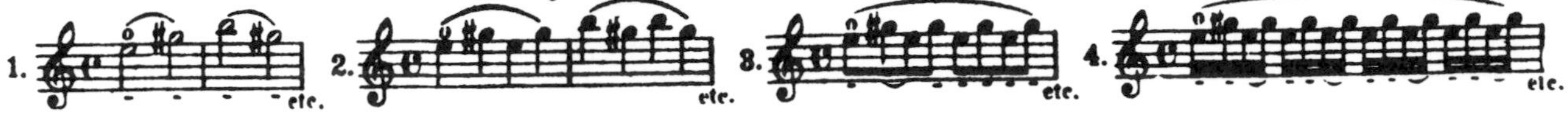

9.

Scale minori armoniche.
Seconda aumentata.
Harmonische Molltonleitern.
Uebermässige Secunde.

Měkké stupnice harmonické.
Zvětšená sekunda.
Gammes mineures harmoniques.
La seconde augmentée.

Гармоническія минорныя гаммы.
Увеличенная секунда.
Harmonic minor scales.
The augmented second.

1. etc. 2. etc. 3. etc. 4. etc.
E moll. – Mi mineur. – mi minore – E moll. – Ми миноръ.
1 tono e ½
1½ Ton.
A moll. – La mineur. – la minore. – A moll. – Ля миноръ.
D moll. – Ré mineur. – re minore. – D moll. – Ре миноръ.
G moll. – Sol mineur. – sol minore. – G moll. – Соль миноръ.
C moll. – Ut mineur. – do minore. – C moll. – До миноръ.
F moll. – Fa mineur. – fa minore. – F moll. – Фа миноръ.
B moll. – Si♭ mineur. – si ♭ minore. – B moll. – Си♭ миноръ.
Es moll. – Mi♭ mineur. – mi ♭ minore. – Es moll. – Ми♭ миноръ.
As moll. – La♭ mineur. – la ♭ minore. – As moll – Ля♭ миноръ.
Gis moll. – Sol ♯ mineur. – sol ♯ minore. – Gis moll. – Соль ♯ миноръ.
Cis moll. – Ut ♯ mineur. – do ♯ minore. – Cis moll. – До ♯ миноръ.
Fis moll. – Fa ♯ mineur. – fa ♯ minore. – Fis moll. – Фа ♯ миноръ.
H moll. – Si mineur. – si minore. – H moll. – Си миноръ.

10.

Accordo di settima sul 5º grado.
Quinta diminuita e quarta aumentata.

Septimenaccord der 5. Stufe.

Verminderte Quinte und übermässige Quarte.

Septimový akkord 5. stupně.
Zmenšená kvinta a zvětšená kvarta.

Accord de septième du 5me degré.
La quinte diminuée et la quarte augmentée.

Септаккордъ 5ой ступени.
Уменьшенная квинта и увеличенная кварта.

Chord of the seventh of the 5th degree
The diminished fifth and the augmented fourth.

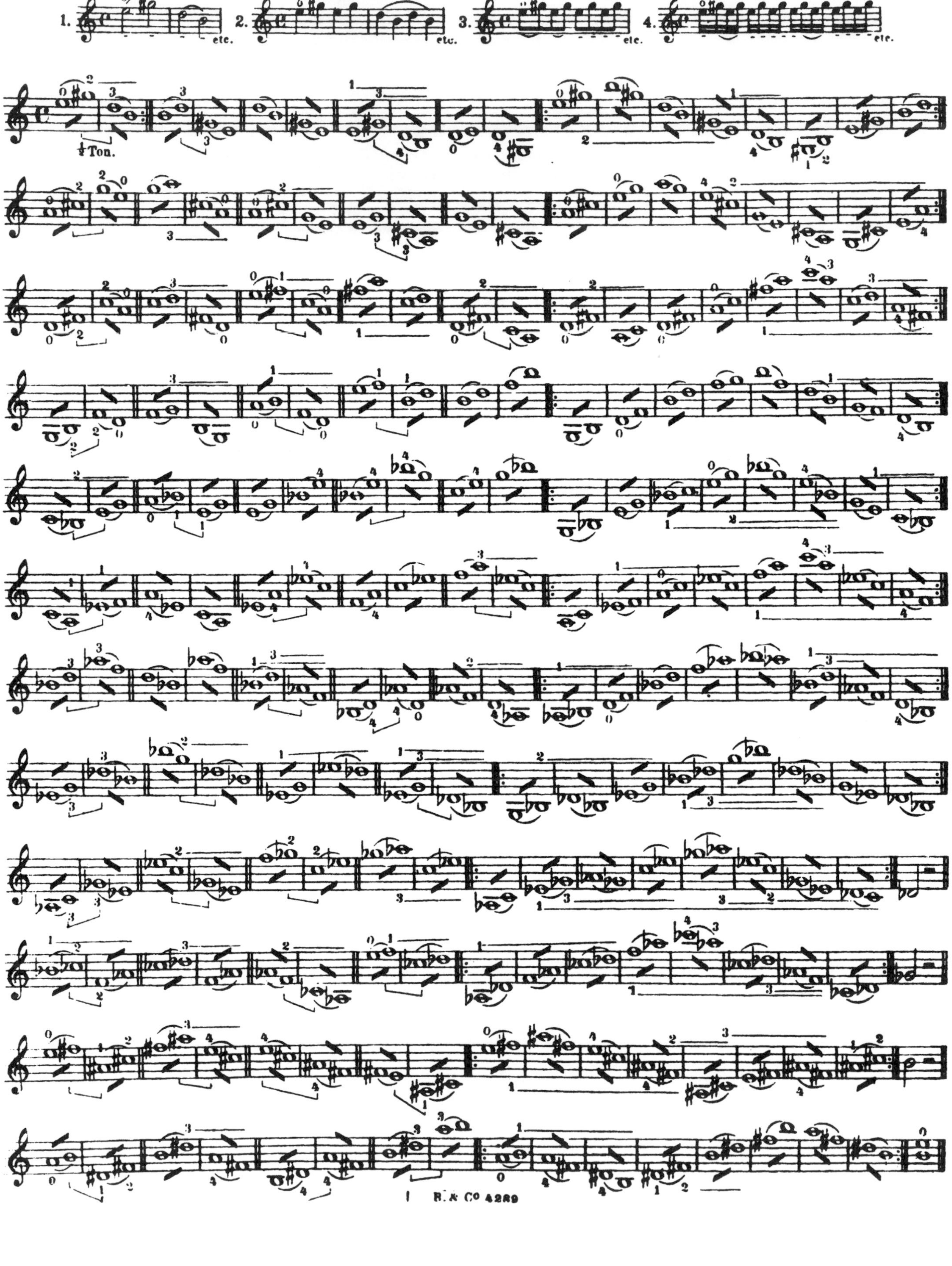

B. & Co 4289

11.

Estensione del 4º dito.
Ausdehnung des 4. Fingers.

Přehmat 4. prstu.
Extension du 4e doigt.

Протяженіе 4го пальца.
Extension of the fourth finger.

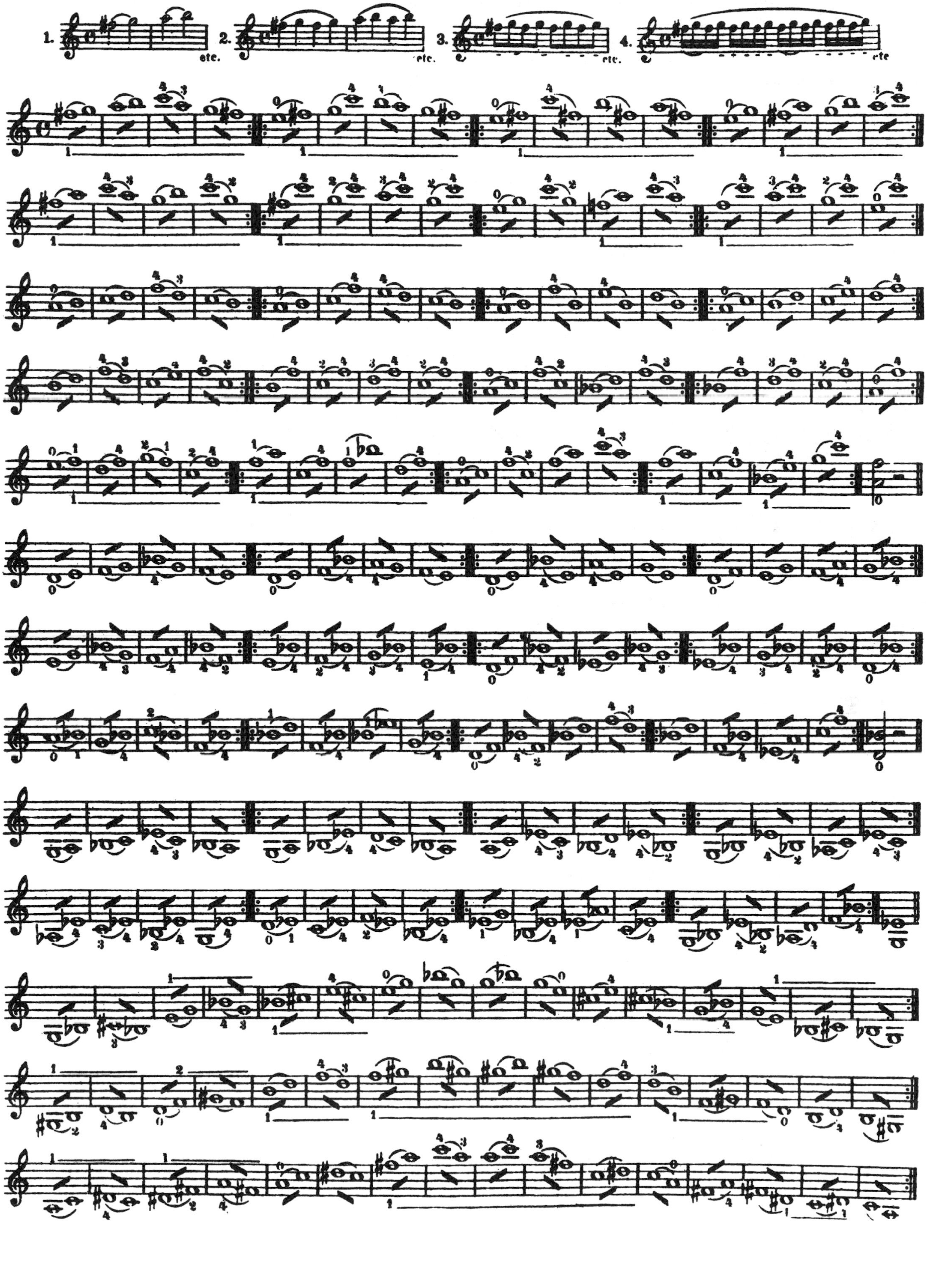

12.

Trillo senza la terminazione.
Triller ohne Nachschlag.

Trilek bez dorážky.
Trille sans terminaison.

Трель безъ заключенія.
Trill without aftertone.

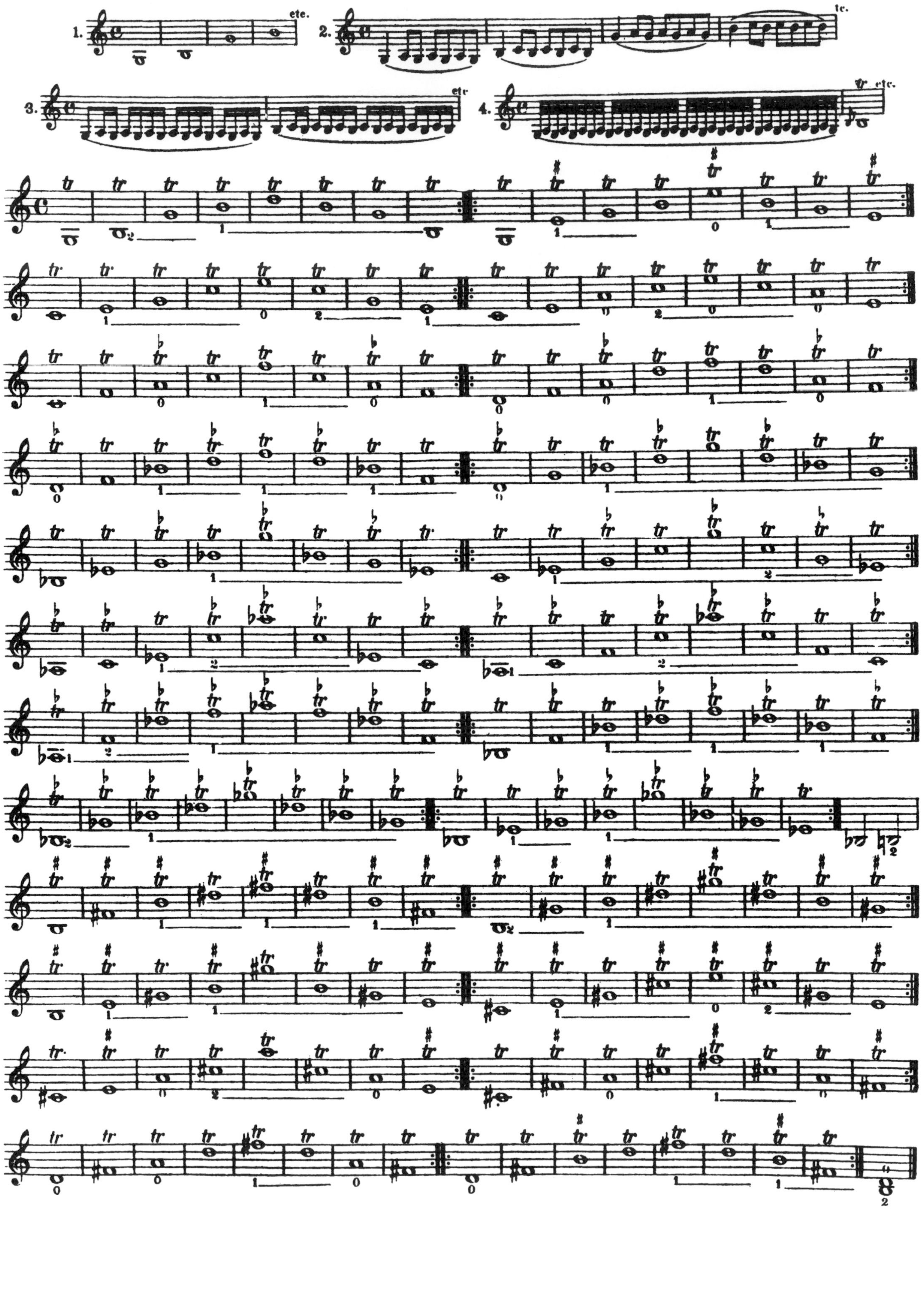

13.

14.

Trillo con la terminazione. | Trilek s dorážkou. | Трель съ заключеніемъ.

Triller mit Nachschlag. | *Trille avec terminaison.* | Trill with aftertone.

tr

15.

16.

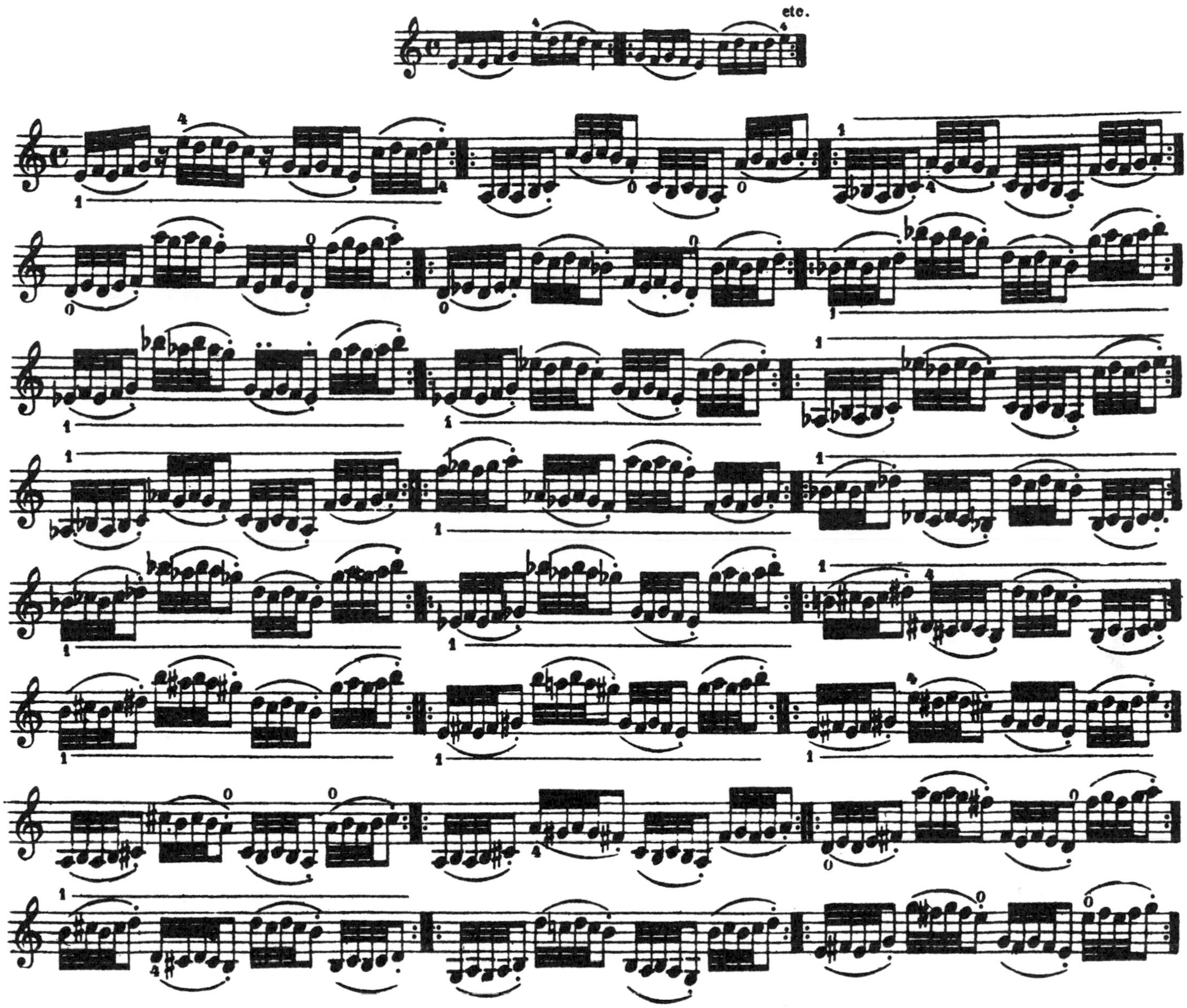

17.

18.

19.

20.

Esercizio di doppie corde.
Accordi perfetti.
Uebung in Doppelgriffen.
Dreiklänge.

Cvičení v dvojhmatech.
Trojzvuky.
Exercice en doubles notes.
Des accords parfaits.

Упражненіе въ двойныхъ нотахъ.
Трезвучія.
Exercise in double notes.
Triads.

21.

Accordo di settima sul 5º grado.
Septimenaccord der 5. Stufe.

Septimový akkord 5 stupně.
Accord de septième du 5. degré.

Септаккордъ 5ой ступени.
Chord of the seventh of the 5th degree.

22.

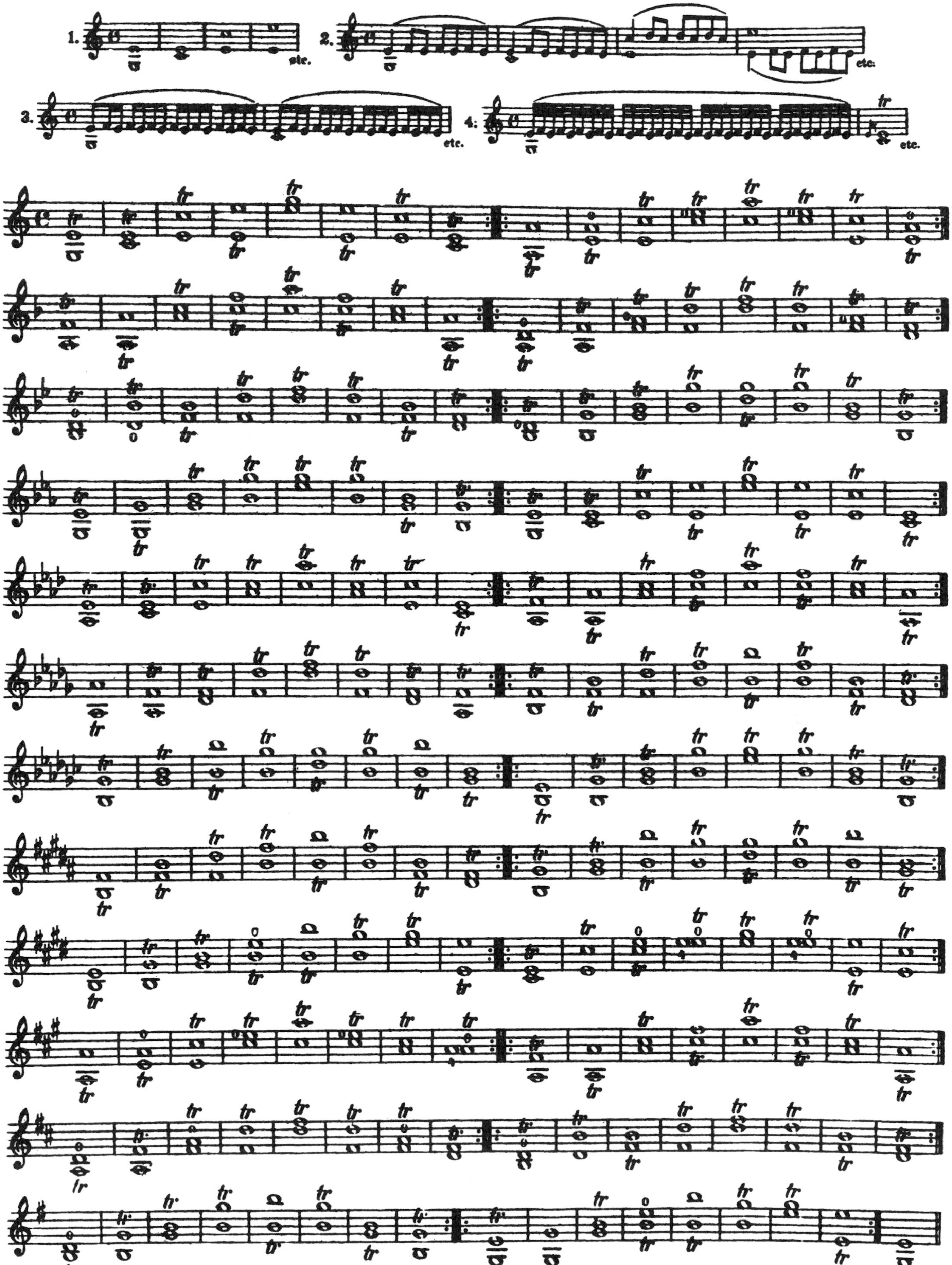

23.

STAGE FRIGHT

ITS CAUSES AND CURES

WITH SPECIAL REFERENCE TO VIOLIN PLAYING

BY

KATO HAVAS

CONTENTS

also by Kato Havas

A NEW APPROACH TO VIOLIN PLAYING
THE TWELVE LESSON COURSE
THE VIOLIN & I